EDGE CITY UK

David Boyle has been writing about new ideas for more than a quarter of a century. He is a former editor of *Town & Country Planning,* co-director of the New Weather Institute, policy director of Radix UK, a fellow of the New Economics Foundation, has stood for Parliament and is a former independent reviewer for the Cabinet Office. He is the author of *Alan Turing, Scandal* and *Before Enigma,* as well as a range of other historical studies. He lives in the South Downs.

Lesley Yarranton is a former journalist, television researcher and translator. She was one of the first western journalists to live in and report from East Berlin after the fall of the Berlin Wall. She has since worked in Paris and Washington DC, where she was a correspondent during the early nineties and witnessed the birth of the first Edge Cities. She lives in the Cotswolds with her family.

# Edge City UK

*Abomination
or new urban form?*

David Boyle
Lesley Yarranton

THE REAL PRESS
www.therealpress.co.uk

Published in 2022 by the Real Press. www.therealpress.co.uk © David Boyle & Lesley Yarranton.

ISBN (print)  978-1912119462
ISBN (ebooks)  978-1912119455

# Acknowledgements

First, we want to thank our main interviewees – Cllr Mike Evans in Whiteley, Cllr David Ellis in Birchwood and the Rev Helen Baker in Graven Hill. We very much appreciate all your help – often at the very last minute. And also our two wise men, David Lock and Olivier Sykes, our two experts.

But equally, we need to thank everyone who has helped us in our journeys around the country – including Fiona Treveil who put us up in Portsmouth, Agatha Treveil and Rob Farrow (and Dougall their dog), who put us up in Graven Hill, and Bernie Rochford, who entertained one of us for an evening between Manchester and Liverpool.

This is also to express our huge love and appreciation to our families in Gloucestershire and West Sussex – without whom none of this would be possible.

*David*
*Lesley*

# Contents

# Foreword

## by Sue Pritchard

*Chief executive of the Food, Farming and Countryside Commission*

This timely text brings a fresh take to a critical question for our time. How shall we live in the 21st century, which provides beautiful, affordable and sustainable housing, in flourishing communities, resilient and adaptable to whatever future scenarios unfold? And who decides?

David and Lesley interrogate a recent answer to that question – Joel Garreau's *Edge City* – contrasting it with UK phenomenon, like the new towns and the garden cities, to see what – if anything – they can offer in answer to that big question.

What is revealing – and disturbing – about the examples that the authors choose is how little 'planning' goes into urban planning these days. Moreover, they illustrate how these big national critical questions about foundational parts of economic and social life are left to an underregulated, heavily subsidised, 'free market' housing sector, who are trousering eye-watering profits, whilst offering ugly, unaffordable, unimaginative, unsafe and insufficient solutions to citizens.

David and Lesley generously point to the work that the Food, Farming and Countryside Commission are doing, on addressing these failings. We advocate for, and are piloting, in Devon and Cambridgeshire so far, a land-use decision making framework which engages communities and stakeholders in transparent, open, inclusive and evidence-led exercises about how land can and should be used - considering things like housing and infrastructure, energy, food and farming, public access, flood mitigations, and for nature recovery and carbon sequestration.

In our work thus far, we find that − far from the popular characterisations of nimbyism or denialism − with the right structures and good information, citizens are very willing and able to engage in these complex questions. They bring creative, pragmatic and ambitious solutions to the table, rooted in their own lived experience of how to make their homes and places work, for now and for future generations.

Designing future-proof places to live, work and be together, that meets peoples' changing needs and gets us back on track to a more sustainable future has to be one of the critical questions of any society. It is one that we need to answer in the UK with fresh urgency.

**Sue Pritchard**
*Chief Executive*
*Food, Farming and Countryside Commission*

# Chapter 1
## *Nowhere City USA*

Just outside Disney World, near Orlando in Florida, you will find the spanking ever-so-wired, futuristic new town of Celebration – the one satirised in the film *Shrek*.

Celebration is the brainchild of Walt Disney himself. He wanted to create a town with a sense of community and cleanliness, but it was put on the company's back burner the moment he died in 1966, and it had to wait to be turned into bricks and mortar by Disney's extremely well-paid CEO Michael Eisner, three decades later.

One clue that there is something a little peculiar about Celebration was partly that it looks scarily like the suburb that imprisoned Jim Carrey in *The Truman Show*, actually filmed in nearby Seaside. Another is the constant repetition in the corporate hype that Celebration is 'real', as if we all need to be reassured about it.

Why might there be any doubt about the reality of Celebration? Well, in the first place, it is probably the first town in the world to have the internet planned in from the start. Celebration is designed specifically as a wired and virtual town – a virtual community, in fact. There are online bulletin boards for everything and an amazing array of online interactivity, delivered by fibre optic network. There is even constant closed circuit TV coverage of what's going on at school which you can watch on the internet.

But what really casts doubt on the reality of the place is the way that it pretends to some kind of permanence. Most of the homes are designed in turn-of-the-century style – the last one – like almost every Disney film you've ever seen. The shops have signs up in the street with bogus foundation dates like 'since 1905' when actually the town and the stores are less than five years old.

It is designed to give a timeless sense of what small town America used to be like – or should have been like – in the days of *It's a Wonderful Life*. Muzak is piped from speakers in the streets, built into the roots of the palm trees. There's a particularly disturbing corner of the town called the 'Preview Centre' which consists simply of full-size pictures of the houses on sale, mounted on billboards – real cardboard cut-outs, in fact.

Disney's brochures call it a "hopscotch-and-tag neighbourhood to be viewed from a front porch wings" and a "special place for families ... in a time of innocence". While we might gag on that kind of saccharine, there is something in this fake place that actually smacks of a new search for something real. There's no Burger King, McDonalds or Wal-mart, as there is in outside most other towns in the USA. It's the only place in the vicinity of Orlando where you can't actually buy Disney World sweatshirts. It may be completely fake, but paradoxically it does seem at least to be in search of something that smacks of the authentic.

No, what really marks Celebration out as worryingly unreal is the involvement of Disney itself, the great reality-managers. Because Celebration is a corporate town. It is there entirely for the greater glory of Disney, and that has some peculiar and unreal implications.

When some of the families complained about standards in the Disney-run Celebration school – a very un-Disney thing to do – the company ignored them and hired a light plane to encourage the principal Bobbi Vogel, who they were afraid had been disheartened by the dispute. It towed a big banner across the town centre bearing the enthusiastic slogan 'Great Job Bobbi' on Celebration's rapidly organised Teacher Appreciation Day.

When some of the families involved decided to pack up and leave, Disney offered to waive the rule that they couldn't profit from the sale if they left in less than a year – but only on condition they signed a contract promising never to reveal their reasons for wanting to go.

There are whole phone directories full of rules for the residents – including one that denies them the right to park pick-up trucks in the street. These can't be changed, even by the elected Homeowners' Association, without the written approval of the company. All power remains behind the scenes with Disney for as long as they want it. Even more peculiar is the attitude of some of the residents to all this. "It's definitely a democracy," one couple told *New York Times Magazine*, "because we can go to the town hall and express our feelings."

That isn't the conventional definition, but then this is *ersatz* consumer democracy rather than the old-fashioned voting kind – and people there don't always seem to be able to tell the difference.

We don't have places like Celebration in the UK, unless you count Prince Charles' *olde worlde* new community of Poundbury in Dorset, which is real in a sense that eludes Celebration. The idea of voluntarily submitting yourself to a code like this may not be either attractive or possible for most of us – who can afford those homes in gated estates, after all? – but it is all the rage in the USA. Because, like Celebration, the so-called Edge Cities are on the march.

And, as we shall see, over here too.

# II

In 1991, the average UK house price was £55,853[1] and a gallon of petrol cost an average £1.80[2]. In September of that year the governor of the Bank of England declared that the country was finally beginning to emerge from the dark of the Gulf War recession. A few weeks later, British workers in the Channel Tunnel glimpsed the flash of torchlight and heard the popping of champagne bottles as they burst through the last dividing chunk of clay.

Prime Minister John Major had just outlined his vision of a "classless Britain". As he was speaking, messages were appearing on the computer screen of British scientist Tim Berners Lee marking the debut of the world's first website.

With auspicious timing, a new book, suggesting a way of adapting to this changing world was published. The dilemma it described was a familiar one: city life had its advantages – easy travel to work, culture, art and restaurants – but also the downsides of expense, crowding, crime and pollution. For most city-dwellers the only alternative was to move out into the anonymous suburbs filled with ribbon housing and retail parks.

---

[1] UK House Price Index - HM Land Registry Open Data.

[2] *http://www.speedlimit.org.uk* › petrolprices.

When American journalist Joel Garreau's *Edge City: Life on the New Frontier* appeared, it pointed to a third option in the shape of what he dubbed the '*retroburb*'.

Garreau, a *Washington Post* journalist, travelled around America chronicling the rise of a new kind of community – distanced from any established town or city yet desirable in its own right, and attractive to dynamic, footloose city-dwellers anxious to preserve that most precious commodity – time. Fed up with a day squeezed between 'dead' travel time, they wanted to move seamlessly between home, work and social life by having everything in one place.

Coining the phrase 'Edge Cities' to differentiate these reinvented suburbs from their much-derided predecessors, Garreau believed they would re-shape our lives by becoming the standard form of urban growth worldwide, rendering our 19th-century post-industrial towns and cities almost obsolete.

"Americans are creating the biggest change in a hundred years in how we build cities," he wrote. He heralded "multiple urban cores" as the "new hearths of civilisation". They did not orbit the traditional city centres as they were their own centres of commerce, residence and recreation – home, workplace and playground" – and were no longer even suburbs, having their own centre of gravity and therefore not deserving the prefix 'sub'.

These new 'civilised' suburbs confounded old traditional, metropolitan thinking. They had no beginning or end, were often sited around motorway junctions, were run by their own independent, quasi governments and by attracting those wearied by life-sapping commutes, promised to become the new energised centres of the nation's real wealth. It would, he suggested, amount to a resettlement of America.

Garreau drew up five basic rules for a place to qualify as one of the frontier 'Edge Cities'.[3] First, as a new "workplace of the Information Age", it needed to have at least five million square feet of office space.

Secondly, it had to offer at least 600,000 square feet of office space for businesses to rent – the equivalent, Jarreau noted, to a "fair-sized mall".

Thirdly, it had to have more jobs than bedrooms so that when the workday started people headed "towards it, not away from it".

Fourthly, that people's perception of it was that it "has it all", from jobs, to shopping to entertainment; it was viewed as a self-contained community rather than as a mere "starting point" for living, working or socialising.

Garreau's fifth and final rule was that it must have sprung from virgin land that, as recently as thirty

---

[3] Joel Garreau: *Edge City, Life on the New Frontier*. 1991. Anchor Books, Doubleday, New York. 7.

years previously, had been "just bedrooms, if not cow pastures".

He went on to list many distinguishing common features of 'Edge Cities', for example how, unlike our nineteenth century urban towns and cities, they often had no clear boundary; "The reason there are no 'Welcome to' signs at Edge City is that it is a judgement call where it begins and ends," he wrote.[4]

They were often governed, not by a recognised authority such as a mayor or city council, but either came under the government of surrounding counties or had their own 'shadow governments' made up of professional and technical bodies.

These communities would have their own, highly visible, private police forces. Safety and the principle of making residents, especially women, feel safe dictated many of the design features such as glass-sided lifts and brightly lit walkways, where "patrol and control" could operate at a high level.

Other hallmarks of an Edge City included the illusion of being close to 'healing' nature: of living, working and enjoying leisure time within a few paces of a 'wildlife refuge'. But far from real wildness, the buildings would be surrounded by well-tended lakes, lawns and jogging trails, and filled with skylights and

---

4 *Ibid.* 6.

atria.[5]

The urge to socialise in these utopian communities was strong. Garreau described their "ultimate value" as being social: "a balance between individualism and face-to-face contact"[6] - noting how people living in Bridgewater Commons in New Jersey were "so hungry for a centre to their Edge City" they waged a two-decade-long campaign for a 'twentieth-century village green'.

"What they wanted was a market meeting place reminiscent of the Greek *agora*. What it turned out to be, of course, was a 900,000-square-foot mall," he reported. But the important point was that "their village square is thriving". The theme of the need for meeting and socialising was one running through interviews given in the wake of the book's launch in the US and struck a chord in Britain.

After one homeowner from Kentlands, an 'Edge City' made up of carefully jumbled traditional, colonial-era style houses with timbered porches, neat lawns and white picket-fences, was interviewed on national television, its developers Andres Duany and Elizabeth Plater-Zyberk were sought out by Prince Charles to assist with the design of Poundbury, his pet-project in Dorset.

---

[5] *Ibid.* 389.

[6] *Ibid.* 42.

Homeowner Stephen Hersh, a 54-year-old psychiatrist had told how people in the 'Traditional Neighbourhood Development' 20 miles north of Washington DC were " in touch with each other. We have town meetings and community groups and newsletters but the real difference is seeing your neighbours every day and talking to them."

But there were criticisms, too, from those unconvinced by Garreau's claim that Edge Cities 'acculturated immigrants'[7] and would reduce 'white flight' from the inner cities. Some saw the movement as merely an excuse for schmaltzy, theme-park architecture, 'McMansions' pandering to the nostalgic twitchings of an insecure middle-class.

"It is an elitist fantasy," said the renowned modern architect, Frank Gehry. "It's like saying to your kids, 'Look, we don't have any new ideas, so we're going to take some from the past." Even the central, retroburban objective of bringing people closer together attracted scepticism. "I grew up in just the kind of old, squiggly-road community that people like Andres Duany hate," says Eve Kahn, architecture critic of the *Wall Street Journal*. "There was a tremendous community there."

But it forced a re-think of our urban future, sparked fresh investigations of demographic shifts

---

[7] *Ibid.* 8.

and brought prescient recognition of the ways in which, long before Covid-19, what Garreau called 'dematerialising technologies' (back then, this meant mobile phones and fax machines), could change the way we lived and worked.[8]

[8] *Ibid*, 133.

# Chapter 2
## *Towards a UK definition*

The idea that some places are more real than others has little by way of intellectual backing. Perhaps it has no meaning at all outside Europe, where places often date back two millennia or more. It certainly was not part of the thesis put forward three decades ago by Joel Garreau. Yet in the UK, it is directly relevant.

Garreau argued that the edge cities have become the standard form of urban growth worldwide, representing a twentieth century urban form. Yet from a European perspective, one of the features which the edge cities lack – clustered around motorway interchanges, or warehouse depots, outside local government jurisdiction – is authenticity. We have no Celebrations in the UK, no corporate realities – thank goodness – but we believe we do now have some edge cities.

Just to remind ourselves, Garreau set out five rules for a place to be considered an edge city:

- It has five million or more square feet (465,000

square metres) of leasable office space.

- It has 600,000 square feet (56,000 sq ms) or more of leasable retail space.
- It has more jobs than bedrooms.
- It is perceived by the population as one place.
- It was nothing like a city as recently as 30 years ago. "Then it was just bedrooms, if not cow pastures."

We believe, for reasons we will explain, that the first three don't apply to Edge City UK. But like the US versions, most of our edge cities have developed at or near existing planned motorway junctions, and are especially likely to develop near major airports. They rarely include heavy industry. They often are not separate legal entities but are governed as part of surrounding counties or district councils.

Garreau identified three distinct varieties of the edge city phenomenon:

1. **Boomburbs** or 'boomers' – the most common type, having developed incrementally but rapidly around a shopping mall or highway interchange, like Tysons in Virginia, outside Washington.

2. **Greenfields** – originally master-planned as new towns, generally on the suburban fringe, for example: Reston, also in Virginia.

3. **Uptowns** – an older city, town, or satellite city, upon and around which a major regional hub of

economic activity rises, for example Arlington, Virginia across the Potomac River from Washington.

It isn't clear yet what the dominant mode of transportation will be in the 21st century. It may not be the motor car – though if it is, then it will be limited by the technological capacity of the electric batteries. Yet Garreau has to be right that edge cities have been driven by traffic and commuting.

Wikipedia lists these other terms which are used to describe edge cities. They include: suburban business districts, major diversified centres, suburban cores, mini-cities, 'suburban activity centers', cities of realms, galactic cities, urban subcentres, pepperoni-pizza cities, superburbia, technoburbs, nucleations, disurbs, service cities, perimeter cities, peripheral centres, urban villages, and suburban downtowns.

These all sound like American phenomena – especially perhaps *technoburbs*. And yet it is our contention that edge cities have begun to emerge in the UK too. We don't mean garden cities or new towns like Letchworth, Welwyn or Milton Keynes, which date back more than a century in the UK. Nor would they include Garreau's third category.

But the first category – the new places that emerge *unplanned*. Yes, we have those, driven as much by the lure of resources as by the roar of traffic.

The main difference between the UK and the USA is that we have a broadly planned environment, partly thanks to the development of new green belts from 1946 and the nationalisation of development rights from the Attlee government onwards, and is in line with the UK tradition as a small, cramped island, compared with the wide open spaces that America boasts.

And yet if you look at our motorway junctions, in some of the fastest growing areas of Britain, there you can see what we think may be emerging edge cities, thanks partly to the decline of planning in the UK.

Edge cities developed in a US context. Starting in the 1950s, businesses were incentivised to open branches in the suburbs and eventually, in many cases, leave traditional downtowns entirely, because of increasing increased use of cars and the move of middle class residents to suburbs, which in turn led to frustration with downtown traffic and lack of parking. And the higher the land values climbed in inner urban areas, the more people moved out.

Despite early examples in the 1920s, it was not until car ownership surged in the 1950s, after four decades of fast, steady growth, that it was possible to move out. US entrepreneurs opened the world's first – and possibly only – drive-thru wedding chapel in Las Vegas in 1951. President Dwight Eisenhower endorsed the interstate highway system five years

21

later, in 1956.

The following decade saw Jack Kerouac's driving novel *On the Road,* plus the opening of Route 66 from Atlantic to Pacific, and slick road movies like *Bullitt.* For the 1950s generation, a car meant freedom from parental control, making out on the back seats at drive-in movies. It meant sexual freedom. You can understand its potency.

It was then, according to Garreau, that edge cities began to emerge on a large scale, first in Detroit's New Center, developed in the 1920s, three miles (5 km) north of downtown, followed by the new Miracle Mile section of Wilshire Boulevard in Los Angeles – one as an office park, the other as a retail strip.

The difference with the UK is that , thanks to rail transport, the British invented suburbs long before before motor traffic – in the early years of the nineteenth century. By 1911, the census showed that most of the big UK cities were losing population from their urban cores.

That in turn led to what the Germans called the 'flight to the green', when those who could afford to leave left the inner cities and often bypassed the suburbs altogether – out to wherever they could afford when Garreau was writing: then still the huge ring around the Home Counties from Norfolk to Dorset, the two fastest growing places in the UK by the 1980s.

This ring was dubbed the Muesli Belt by Martin Stott in his 1988 style guide *Spilling the Beans,* with his tongue firmly in his cheek. Though we could not help noticing that, in the 1989 elections for the European parliament – a political nadir for the Lib Dems – the Greens came second right along the muesli belt and nowhere else. The Belt was really there.

The previous year, the geography and population team led by Tony Champion at Newcastle University revealed for the first time since before World War I that the populations of the UK big cities were growing again. Liverpool had lost a third of its population since World War II – it hardly seemed possible that engine would ever go into reverse. Yet it has done.

It was partly the expansion of higher education and perhaps higher migration. Sadly, the days of the muesli belt were also over, because higher house prices have undermined the chances for downshifters to afford them any more. Instead they must go north or west or to places like Hay-on-Wye, but they don't otherwise cluster.

Apart from that UK land use has been subject to the same kind of pressures as they have in the USA, especially as UK planning has been seriously diminished – both in reputation and in their budgets and remit. The result has been a similar phenomenon to the one Garreau recorded in the USA, but our edge cites – which we are tempted to call *nowhere cities* here – are truly fake. They were not planned by anybody. Often, they are just dormitory towns for commuters, perhaps around distribution centres, near one of the key motorway corridors, like the M11 or the M27.

They often have no name, except perhaps among the estate agent fraternity, but they are there, nonetheless.

We are also a good deal less enthusiastic about Nowhere City than Garreau was about Edge City.

Today, many US edge cities have plans for densification, sometimes around a walkable downtown-style core, often with a push for more accessibility by transit and bicycle, and addition of housing in denser, urban-style neighbourhoods within the edge city. For example at Tysons, in the Washington DC metro area, the plan remains to see the city become the downtown core of Fairfax County.

Other cities around the world are sporting office buildings in their outskirts too. But there is a question mark after Covid over the future of offices.

There has been a considerable debate among economists as to whether "jobs follow people or people follow jobs", but in the context of the edge city phenomenon, workers have been drawn from metropolitan business hubs in favour of the edge city economies.

Garreau states one reason for the rise of edge cities is that: "Today, we have moved our means of creating wealth, the essence of urbanism – our jobs – out to where most of us have lived and shopped for two generations. That has led to the rise of Edge City.[9]

In comparison with traditional urban centres, edge cities offer global corporations many advantages: cheaper land, security, efficient land communications, advanced technological installations, and a high quality of life for their employees and executives, says Garreau. They also appear to offer more space and flexibility, and in the US context, less racism. Our investigation will decide if the same is true in the UK.

That is why, when *Edge City* emerged exactly 30 years ago, it caused such a stir. "Readable... a fascinating transcontinental tour" wrote one critic, "Mr Garreau has the ability to categorise and clarify trends before they are apparent to the rest of us. His instincts are sharp, and his arguments are often persuasive... *Edge City* ... is a provocative introduction to demographic and business patterns that are likely to become more important as the twenty-first century edges nearer."

---

[9] ."https://en.wikipedia.org/wiki/Edge_city_-_cite_note-:2-19

# II

So this is our updated but tentative definition of Edge City UK, based on what Garreau wrote – but written before we went out to find UK examples. See if you recognise it...

1.  It was built around 10-30 miles away from a big city and has offices, shops and residential buildings close by, but the actual city has more offices than beds. People who work in it often live close by.

2.  It may not have a mayor or any local council type of government.

3.  It 'acculturates' immigrants (this might just be an American thing but worth looking at). In the USA, edge cities were very good for black middle-class.

4.  It has moved away from areas where raw materials could be made into useful products (the traditional city model)

5.  It might have warehouses (Amazon?).

6.  It might have gyms, yoga halls and cinemas.

7.  It probably has big or high-rise office buildings – lots of corporate glass and steel – where the only time you ever see anyone is in the lift.

8.  It should be a place where old people live and come out to exercise in the morning, because it challenges the idea that cities are best for the young.

9.  It has high-class security and no crime – no dark alleyways – but this means very little 'truly' public space.

10.   It will have lawns and some connection to wildlife – wooded walkways, a lake or jogging tracks but all these connections utterly 'tamed' – so no spontaneity.

11.  It will probably be situated close to motorway junctions or where two motorways intersect and have good schools nearby.

12.  It may have erased a historic location where people used to have a sense of 'clear identity'.

13.  People or companies who moved to it did so to conserve what Garreau calls 'our most precious commodity – time'.

14.  It boosted shops in the area as people were no longer having to commute to the big city 30 or so miles away.

15.  Its creation was developer-driven – with little or no input from architects.

16.  Garreau talks about London's edge cities being off the M11, M25 and M20.

17.  It was built to create a 'sense of community', but has probably failed due to lack of '*us*-ness'.

18. It was built around the use of cars.

19. It may have a lifespan of no more than 25 years. A new generation will have grown up in it but will have a 'different life'.

20.  Its design was founded in America on the premise that the furthest an American would willingly walk before getting into a car (at time of publication – probably less now) was just 600 feet.

# Chapter 3

## *Security city: Whiteley*

We discovered Whiteley when we were driving along the M27 with Fiona, David's sister, who used to work there (she wasn't a fan). You could see it poking out above the trees as we drove by. We noticed it wasn't on our elderly map.

The M27 is one of those motorways that the Department of Transport, on the run from environmental activist Swampy and his friends in the mid-1990s, was trying to build furtively all the way along the south coast of England. That is why only one particularly busy section has been labelled as such, snaking along between Portsmouth, Southampton and the New Forest.

The whole way along the M27, and especially to the north, there are possible future edge cities. Then suddenly at Junction 9 – between Portsmouth and Eastleigh – there is a four-lane highway driving off the motorway, apparently into the woods. Follow it and you find yourself in the heart of Whiteley's business district – by the dwindling headquarters of big names like HSBC, Zurich and Specsavers.

It peters out in what looks like a beautiful and enticing woodland walk and stream. All around us are tinted office windows and acres of empty tarmac where the employees used to park before Covid. And for some reason, so many ambulance staff – it transpires that they have been taking part in some kind of exercise.

This is one indication that we are in an edge city – the amount of office space relative to residential space is part of the original American definition. But there is another reason too. Whiteley straddles two district council areas – Fareham to the east and Winchester to the north. We heard later that this is also a kind of class divide in leafy Whiteley between the two districts.

There was a fascinating confusion about when it all began. "Whiteley started 23 years ago – before I was born," said the young woman in one local estate agency definitively and with unexpected precision.

When we went to see the chair of Whiteley Town Council, Mike Evans, he pushed the start date back about four years, to 1994. "When we were granted a new parish council," he said.

Zurich made their UK headquarters there a little later. HSBC moved there from Southampton. Then came NATS, the national air traffic controllers; not to mention Specsavers.

There are two contradictory stories about year zero if you look up Whiteley in Wikipedia: when the first buildings appeared on site - either the Solent Hotel in the early 1990s. Or was it the first houses built there – even before the publication of *Edge City* in 1991. Perhaps we need to go back even further to 1977, when the houses first appeared in the Hampshire structure plan.

Still, the fact is that here is Whiteley – nobody really planned it like this (unless it was British Land, which plays Disney's role in Celebration), yet it has its own sports centre and town council, with its own coat of arms (a deer, a family and an oak tree).

The real beating heart of the town is the new £100m shopping development by British Land, which began in 2007 with the demolition of the old shopping centre, Whiteley Shopping Village (except for Tesco, which is still there). And then opening it again in 2011 with the help of Denise Van Outen. Not to mention a new nine-screen cinema.

We sit outside Costa Coffee – there are no locally owned brands here at all. No small shops, which is some measure of how vulnerable the Whiteley economy might be if British Land was less than happy (small shops probably can't afford the rents).

It is a warm day and shortly after the third lockdown, but the place is quite busy. Everyone seems rather plumper than others living in south Hampshire, and for whom body image is all-important. Though that is a positive as far as David is concerned...

Unlike most other shopping centres in the country, this one has virtually no vacancies and it is also fitted with pleasant wooden cladding. Plus as many as 96 security cameras. You are very seriously watched when you go shopping here – as you might expect in Security City.

Because this isn't just home to many ambulances, nor NATS – Whiteley is also where you can find the headquarters of Special Branch.

Appropriately enough, the town council chair Mike is a bronzed, golf-playing former security man. His career took him via the Ministry of Defence, to Afghanistan and then Australia. He took early retirement to avoid going back to Afghanistan, but not before moving to Whiteley.

The town was emerging mainly in the southern parishes of Winchester. There are now 18,000 people living there, and more on the way, now that 3,500 houses are emerging slowly south of the Botley Road, mainly in the western parishes of Fareham.

"When I got here, only 400 families had moved in," Mike tells us.

It hardly needs saying that many of them were military families, and a lot of policeman, plus air traffic controllers.

"It is very popular with families," says Mike.

But the shopping centre and cinema have become a major draw beyond the locals. A terrifying 7 million came during the year before lockdown, lured there by four hours of free parking.

If you ignore the design of some of the houses around the shopping centre, which look as if they have been chopped in half from above, this is clearly a good, *secure* place to bring up families. It is calm, well-ordered, exemplary, to quote Mr Banks in *Mary Poppins,* as if somebody has been cutting the grass verges with nails scissors, just like in Celebration.

There are 88 hectares of woodland, which the town council now manages. So why do we both get a strong sense that it would be a great pity if everywhere in the UK was going to be like Whiteley?

First, because there is no history, apart from the name – taken from what had once been a local farm – and a faint memory of allied troops before D-Day, hiding in the woods, to avoid giving the game away about the Calais route for invasion. It feels like a one-dimensional place.

Second, that there is something a little bit worrying about living with 96 cameras in the shopping centre. That seems to me to be taking security a little bit far. Yet it is probably a one side-effect of the security mindset, given that – actually, there are few police on duty here and the jewellers was recently broken into at night.

Finally, and not the least, there is the obvious problem about traffic, especially during the rush hour, as Fiona had told us. In fact, Mike confirmed that, before lockdown, you needed to leave town straight after lunch or risk getting stuck in your own office until nightfall.

"Really, you had to leave by 2pm or you wouldn't get out," says Mike.

What is more, this can only get worse now another 3,500 homes are taking shape on green fields to take the town up to Botley station in the north. That development will bring with it a new bus route, but otherwise there are no buses at all serving the centre – and it is probably just too far to walk either from Botley or from Swanwick station in the south, just on the other side of the motorway.

So as many as 85 per cent of the visitors come by car. Even during the height of the pandemic, people still drove in to buy coffee, and from as far away as Gosport.

# II

The traffic problem remains the big one and it is hard to see how they might avoid it. This truly is an example of the limits to growth.

It seems obvious to them that they need more parking space in town, but the new arrivals particularly object. And in any case, the real constraint is the motorway, which – as in so many cases – is getting an extra lane in what was the emergency lane. But after that, where?

They have a new secondary school now building, and two new primary schools – one of them closing and opening on a new site the following September.

The town council organises two events every year: their annual music festival and annual fireworks display both attract 9,000 people.

The problem Whiteley has is that its continued success is predicated on it carrying on growing. You do have to ask what would happen, for example, if British Land got bored of shopping malls, as people have in the USA. Or if people stopped working in offices permanently.

"We have asked the question, if these buildings stay empty," says Mike. But he doesn't think that is likely and – who knows? – he could be right.

Meanwhile, Whiteley braces itself for the new influx of population.

"There is very little social housing, some on the Fareham side," Mike tells us. "A few of them have come from the bad parts of Gosport, which has caused some problems. The face of Whiteley is

35

changing and we don't know what the new residents will be like."

Shock! The bad parts of Gosport must send a shiver down the spine of the security-minded – but there is no doubt that Whiteley works, for now...

It is just that its future would hang in the balance in a different kind of world.

# Chapter 4
## *Science city: Birchwood*

*"The surface, at a distance, looks black and dirty, and will bear neither horse nor man... What nature meant by such a useless production 'tis hard to imagine, but the land is entirely to waste."*

That was the rather downright verdict of the great writer Daniel Defoe, as he rode through the place then known as Risley in 1724.

These days, the land between Liverpool and Manchester is still difficult to navigate, mainly because it is urban sprawl of a kind that tends to grow up along the first steam passenger journey in the world. Though Risley was nearly always an exception because - during the Second World War – it became a huge armaments factory on 27 acres between Leigh and Warrington.

As so often with edge cities, this meant that they were on the borderland. Before the war, both Leigh and Warrington were in Lancashire. Now they are in the nether world between Greater Manchester and Cheshire.

The Royal Ordnance Factory was built there because of Risley's local reputation for mist and fog. Even in the daytime, it was supposed to be all but invisible from the air. This is now the site for one of the most famous edge cities in the UK. It is now called *Birchwood*.

Immediately before the Second World War, Risley Royal Ordnance Factory (ROF) was a filling factory. It received the explosives in bulk, usually by rail, from other ROFs where they were made. Risley specialised in filling them into the various casings to produce the finished munitions. There were 16 filling factories around the country and Risley was known as Filling Factory No. 6.

One of the features common to all of the filling factories was an area of storage bunkers where the finished munitions were stored awaiting dispatch. The areas within the filling factories were all numbered in the same way.

Storage bunkers were designated as Area 9. Risley had 20 of these, and four of them can still be seen – strange dinosaurs to survive the closure of the site after VE Day in 1945.

But the site didn't stay quiet for long. A few months later, in January 1946, the Directorate for Atomic Energy Production was set up by the Ministry of Supply under Lord Hinton of Bankside – who chose Risley as his headquarters. The purpose was to provide the plutonium, and anything else required to build a British A-bomb. It was to be the biggest and most expensive UK scientific undertaking, and it needed the involvement of most of the country's top scientists, plus an enormous budget.

There was even its own railway link to Manchester to bring in staff from there. Once the UK Atomic Energy Authority had been launched in 1954 – ahead of the government's announcement that it would build an H-bomb the following year - the AEA employed more than 20,000 people, most of them at Risley. This figure soon doubled.

When the AEA moved its operations to Harwell in Oxfordshire, the disused Risley site was put up for sale in 1963. It slowly overgrew for five years when the new Warrington Development Corporation bought the site and called it 'Birchwood'.

# II

Now, we would like to distinguish new towns like Warrington and garden cities like Welwyn from edge cities like Birchwood, though there is clearly more than a small overlap. The growth of Warrington was managed by a new town development corporation, designated in 1968 – a third generation new town, along with Peterborough, Telford and Milton Keynes, though the development corporation model was invented by the Attlee government, based on the legal structure of the BBC, which had in turn been modelled by Lord Reith on the London Passenger Transport Board.

They had major powers of compulsory purchase – to buy land at 'existing use value' – which meant they could multiply its value ten times over just by giving themselves planning permission. This 'betterment' – as planners call it – paid for cleaning up the other infrastructure.

The basic idea came from a House of Commons shorthand writer with a lugubrious white moustache called Ebenezer Howard, who bought the sites for the first two garden cities, Welwyn and Letchworth, in the early years of the twentieth century. But by the time a group of students took over Stevenage station in 1947 and changed the signs to Silkingrad – a reference to the planning minister, Lewis Silkin – the idea of new towns had become a great deal bigger, rather than better.

The final stage of new towns – designated in 1968 and including – redeemed the idea in the eyes of the public (and in ours!).

So when Warrington and Runcorn Development Corporation was in place, one of their first decisions was to extend their area by snapping up the overgrown Risley site.

So why is Birchwood, as the area came to be called, an edge city, rather than simply an officially designated suburb of Warrington? Partly because it on the opposite side of the M6, near the interchange with the M62 – and the statue known as the 'Angel of Birchwood'. And partly because it has its own elected town council too.

It is all a little ambiguous.

But from our point of view there was another reason we had to include Birchwood – because most of the geographers we interviewed all mentioned it as a key edge city in the north.

# III

We arrived in Birchwood centre by taxi from Warrington North railway station – through unexpectedly busy streets (this was soon after the end of the final lockdown of 2021).

After the traffic in Warrington, Birchwood felt completely deserted. There was an enormous artificial lake, with a huge wooden terrace and lunch bar. It was also lunchtime, but the bar was shut and the terrace was empty there. A couple of people descended sedately from buses, but that was all. The huge car parks were empty too – it felt a little like a great deserted university in the depths of the summer months or long vacation.

In short, despite the vigour of other edge cities we have seen, this one reeked of the public sector – it all just felt a little too careful.

We were due to meet a local councillor David Ellis, who represented Birchwood for Labour on Warrington Borough Council, but was also an elected member of the town council.

We sat down in the terrace of a huge pentagon-shaped red-brick office block – nobody seemed to be working in any of the offices. Perhaps they sat here to plan Calder Hall – the first nuclear power station in the UK, we wondered.

When we go to an edge city, we always tend to ask the same key question: what kind of people live here? We asked David Ellis exactly that, and this is what he said:

"We have an unusual population in Birchwood, because we have between 20 and 30 per cent living in social housing – but we also have the highest proportion of higher degrees in the country. A lot of people have retired, so we also have a large number of well-educated older people."

David told us there was a higher proportion of scientific PhDs living and working there than anywhere else in the country. This was a somewhat scary thought – though there were clearly few enough of them around then.

In fact, Birchwood's population of over 11,200 is rather well-off, compared to other northern towns. About 65 per cent of the 5,000 homes here are owner-occupied – and worth on average only about £115,000 – with as many as 28 per cent renting from the local authority, plus and about 5 per cent renting from somewhere else.

Again, a major difference with American edge cities is that this isn't the kind of place where the black middle classes have flocked to – on the grounds that they are less likely to have developed racist tramlines of thought. In fact, an amazing 97 per cent are white. There is an average age of 37.

"Not many people move away from Birchwood," David Ellis told us. "When you look at our street, those who aren't there any more have mainly died. Housing is relatively cheap but it's a green sort of area – with lots of opportunities for walking – which is why it can be hard to move away."

There must have been a number of professional people working here in the elderly looking red brick offices where we sat with David in the courtyard in the middle of Birchwood – but there still appeared to be nobody there.

There was also something faintly antiseptic about it, with its perfectly cut grass and empty car parks.

"We loved it when we arrived back in 1984," he tells us. "It's a great place to live in in many ways – there are a lot of green areas and parks. You definitely feel outside the big cities here."

# IV

Dave Ellis very kindly says he can take us on a small tour of the town on the way to the shopping centre and the railway station.

We are soon driving by each of the three townships, and then you can really begin to see the relevance of the 'Birchwood' name. The main feeling we get is the sense that this town is about to be overwhelmed by wild brush and undergrowth, huge tentacles of brambles threaten every roundabout and every gap between homes.

There is a wildness about this place, and it derives from nature. This isn't the kind of fake wildness you get in the antiseptic American edge cities – it *felt* real.

Though, you can equally well see the concrete reminders that this was once a place for handling explosives.

We drove around the town, those parts not yet overwhelmed by the encroaching forest. There was no huge difference in the architecture between those townships with more social housing and those with little – unfortunately, it is usually possible to tell most social housing built by the private sector because it looks a little more rickety than the others and, when it is built by the public sector, the front doors tend to be right next door to each other – as if forcing tenants into some kind of relationship with each other.

Sadly, it can have the opposite effect. It was still hard to discern around here.

Even so – perhaps because the forest threatens everyone – all three townships felt similar. He precise stratification of posher Gorse Covert, Locking Stumps through to slightly less posh Oakwood is not really obvious from its architecture.

Birchwood is a relatively mature edge city – there are three primary schools already running – one for each township, and a high school and a community college next door to it in Oakwood.

They each have, not just a primary school and a village shop-cum-post office, but their own pub. Maybe you can read something into the names of these - from the Poacher (Gorse Covert), the Turf and Feather (Locking Stumps) to Nelsons Quarterdeck (Oakwood). Even so, we're not sure you can.

We asked about class tensions in Birchwood.

"That is a very interesting question," he said, then immediately afterwards he dampened our hopes:

"But I guess there isn't...."

"Because I have to cross the main road to get between Locking Stumps and Oakwood, it may be that we don't mix as much as we think. You see, they both have a kind of sense of belonging. But divisions? I don't think there is such a thing. There is a good sense of community here.'"

Now there were certainly trees everywhere , but – when we first arrived – every new drawing was marked by extra lawns and trees, to encourage people to invest there.

David Ellis sees Birchwood slightly differently from Warrington next door, under whose powerful town hall in the new town centre David's parish council draws its power from – and most of its money too. It is set between two motorways, the M6 and the M62 – and the old line is still there underneath the modern railway track between Liverpool and Manchester.

Lockdown was a big problem for Birchwood – and you can see how it might have been with its population of retired scientists "We had to close two local charities, and – because of the work they used to do, this has had a devastating effect."

One of those two charities was directing local advisors to give advice on how to deal with applications to the Benefits Agency or the DWP.

Then suddenly, we were in the town centre, a huge

area of concrete with the shopping centre in the heart of it. This was about as different as it is possible to be from the brand new and expensive 'clone' shopping centre in Whiteley in relatively plush Hampshire.

We walked through it. There were not that many people around, although it was only mid-afternoon. The only crossovers of retail tenants with Whiteley were Costa and Timpsons, the key cutters. Yes, they had Greggs, Aldi and Asda (they may be a little downmarket for Whiteley).

They also had a number of local chains, like Home Bargains ("top brands, bottom prices"), Indigo Sun ("for all your tanning needs") and Oops! ("we prevent food from being wasted by repacking food that is perfectly safe to eat but may have ended up in the clearance section").

# V

Heading out of Birchwood was relatively simple. Public transport is plentiful and inexpensive in this area - as you might expect from an area once served by the first passenger railway service in the world – and we were heading on to Rainhill in fact, to see a friend. This was the scene of the Rainhill Trials two centuries ago, which decided on Stephenson's *Rocket* to pull the train (and where the minister in charge

William Huskisson was knocked down and killed by the winning engine).

We looked out of town from the platform of Birchwood railway station, and saw the wheat waving in the breeze, as far as the eye could see across rural Lancashire. The railway was the very edge of town.

This is a place that takes transport seriously. There are not just two motorways and – from 1981 – the railway station. There are also no less than six bus routes that include Birchwood, plus their own local bus that, in normal times, ferries the commuters to the red-brick pentagon where we had first met David.

What we felt about Birchwood was that it seemed unexpectedly alien – perhaps because we are southerners and the north-south divide has been growing decade by decade throughout our adult lives.

There is also something a little unnerving about visiting the very place where they designed the H-bomb and Windscale, the nuclear reprocessing plant, and other horrors of the 1950s.

At least, though, you can escape easily if you want to – if you can slip out of the embrace of the brambles.

# Chapter 5
## *Self-build city: Graven Hill*

In the years after World War II, America invented modern suburbia, but also created the stigma of living there.

A similar pattern of movement emerged in Britain. It was mostly the penny-pinching, the indifferent and the thick-skinned who responded with enthusiasm to making the suburbs their home. The absence of pubs, cultural venues and meeting places made it seem as if human contact had been virtually designed out of these new-built rows of identikit homes.

The new 'countryside cities' Garreau saw springing into life "like dandelions across America's fruited plains in the 90s" were rooted in the drive to replace suburban isolation with a strong sense of community.

He found "disparate people seeking connectedness", desperate to carve out a "sense of *us*-ness" amid blank, unfeeling, anonymous surroundings.[10]

The same yearning for 'strength of community' voiced by Garreau's Edge City pioneers thirty years ago is echoed by those who have made their homes in one of Britain's first large-scale self-build village: Graven Hill, near Bicester in Oxfordshire.

The scheme was conceived eight years ago when Cherwell District Council was offered the chance to buy hundreds of acres of Ministry of Defence land on its doorstep. The site had played a strategic wartime role as ordnance storage depot, but when the military pulled out, it fell into disuse.

In 2014, the council bought part of the land for £28 million but instead of selling it to developers they loosened mainstream planning regulations and – in a ground-breaking experiment – agreed to sell up to 1,900 plots of land within the next decade, offering buyers the possibility of literally building a home from scratch.

Most hire help from architects then manage with help from builders what they cannot achieve in a television 'Grand Designs' style project. Others with less energy, time and money buy a plot of land then fit out a ready-made shell.

This radical move paid off. Once-incorrigible 'townies', many disillusioned at the prospect of being

---

[10] *Ibid,* 282.

locked into an endless chain of housing-market moves, leapt at the chance of building their dream home in the countryside. Why struggle to do up a draughty Victorian semi when you can design your own modern, personalised, 'forever' light-filled space complete with underfloor heating from an air source heat pump?

But beyond the wish for a home in your image, it is the attraction of sharing a lifestyle with similarly minded neighbours that is fast turning Graven Hill into something the Americans would probably term an *'ecoburb'*. Certainly, much of the talk about Graven Hill becoming a 'strong, environmentally-conscious community' echoes the *'us*-ness' of their Edge City forbears of thirty years ago.

Graven Hill's 'community minister' Helen Baker summed up the attraction of the site:

"People who are engaged here have a strong sense of community and that means they do largely want a lot of what they're looking for in life to come from here, particularly because they have built their own houses.

Their houses are everything they want a home to be and they're invested in making the community what they want it to be. They feel really strongly about their friendships and social time and knowing their neighbours, sharing the space, meeting up with people."

Her words echo those of a resident of Kentlands, an American edge city built on an old northern Virginian farmstead in 1988, offering a range of house designs though none of them self-build. Interviewed about his move away from the city, the 54-year-old clinical psychiatrist Stephen Hersh said: "Here, things are different. The focus is on getting along together. People are in touch with each other. We have town meetings and community groups and newsletters, but the real difference is seeing your neighbours every day and talking to them."

Residents point to the attraction of 'walkable' countryside while remaining within easy distance of friends and relatives. With the 160 designer-name fashionable boutiques and food outlets of Bicester Village as well as an historic market town centre on the doorstep, Graven Hill had a degree of separateness long before improving 'self-containment' was written into the local plan as a 'central strategy'.

The residents of Graven Hill have made it clear that they want to walk to their local shops, pub and community centre as well.

"There are quite strong feelings about what shops there are going to be and where the pub and community centre will be sited," says Baker who notes that a lot more people are working from home since the pandemic began.

The desire to remain within easy reach of friends and relatives is clear. Lying in the centre of the country, bounded by the M40 and two railway stations, Graven Hill lies just 14 miles from Oxford and under an hour from London and has the added advantage of connections to the five counties of the Oxford-Cambridge arc.

Cancer researcher Agatha Treveil and her data engineer partner, Rob Farrow, who moved from Norwich to manage a self-build home there last year, said: "We found Bicester to be a really great location for the trade off between ease of travel to Oxford and London and cost of living there.

The 28-year-old travels to work in Abingdon by car twice a week. Rob, 29, cycles the six minutes to the station to take the train to London twice a week.

"Wanting to stay in the mid/south area of the country, where all our family and friends live, while giving ourselves lots of current and future job opportunities was also a priority," says Agatha. "I worked out that, with friends and family in Hampshire, Kent, London, Surrey, West Sussex, Northamptonshire, Buckinghamshire and Norfolk, we can travel to all of them in 2.5 hours or less. I certainly couldn't say that about living in Norwich."

Like many of the couples moving to Graven Hill,

53

their perspective is long term. Though they chose to build a smaller house ("a larger house uses more building materials, energy to heat, involves more land and results in the inevitable collection of more material wealth which we wanted to avoid") its upstairs area can be easily subdivided into childrens' bedrooms enabling them to start a family without having to move.

"Moving house is extremely expensive, time consuming and disruptive and I do not want to have to do that again for a long time. If kids come along then of course it's best for them to have stability and not need to move. Plus, both Rob and I are a bit bored of moving to a new county every few years, just as you start to really integrate."

Other Graven Hill residents have similarly 'future-proofed' by designing in space for lifts or ground floor extensions for the years when age begins to take its toll or there is a need for elderly relatives can move in.

As Baker puts it: "There's an understanding of wanting to stay here as the family develops, grows, recedes and changes."

She was given the title 'community minister' when she was appointed by Bicester's Orchard Baptist Church in November 2018. She lived offsite until her own self-build home was ready, moved in March 2020, and was immediately confronted with the challenge of lockdown. She says she spent some of this time 'listening' and what she heard was a strong desire to 'belong'.

'People feel really strongly about their friendships and social time and knowing their neighbours, sharing the space, meeting up with people. I think that is a really important part of what they want to happen here.

"I think they are fed up with that sense of not knowing their neighbours and their neighbourhood and not feeling a part of something. That's something we've lost in the last however many decades but now there's a real shift, and people are recognising that they have lost something."

Graven Hill is designed for a cosy, 'community feel' with narrow walkways criss-crossing the streets to give an old-fashioned 'squiggly-road' impression. But Baker knows this is not enough to guarantee community bonds.

She believes that by fostering an inclusive society at an early stage of a community's growth it can become 'baked in' as it grows (there are currently 400 occupations). "If you set the culture at the beginning you hope it follows through, whereas if a community is formed in a vacuum, you can't form the kind of culture you want."

To this end she has created three 'open-to-all groups' around common interests: a gardening club, a toddler group and a choir. She is also in the process of setting up a mental health wellbeing café.

It has not all been plain sailing. Despite efforts to break down barriers, between what could be termed an 'eco-elite' and those receiving food bank parcels, social division has inevitably seeped in. Book club literary discussion is far from a 'must-have' for those who would rather have a well-stocked clothing exchange.

"For me, personally, the social mixing is the one thing that hasn't been overcome," says Baker. "The kind of people who choose to move here, certainly the self-build community, they're 'do-ers', make-it-happeners, and they will overcome the problems. The difficulty is they don't really consider the whole community... they mostly consider themselves.

"A sort of subconscious social divide is in existence even at this early stage.

In some residents' language there is an 'us/them' kind of mentality."

Her efforts have been further frustrated by the Graven Hill development company. She remains critical of the way 'unimaginative' social housing was grouped apart from other housing and given a nearly identical character. The developers also changed the masterplan – initially without consultation – to relocate the proposed pub and community hub from a central site to a less prominent one.

Even her request for a Christmas tree for residents to sing carols around was rejected after falling foul of the developers' 'plant police'.

Undeterred, the residents would "sing anyway", she says cheerfully. She concedes that the project has been a steep learning curve for developers more used to handing over 'ready-made' estates.

"This is the first self-build community in the UK and no building company has ever had to deal with residents living on site while they are being built around and then wanting to have some ownership of their community," she explains. They are used to having full control but you can't treat this building development in the same way you would treat any other because it isn't the same – you haven't built 500 houses, moved 500 families in and then said: 'This is what you've got' – you've moved 20 families in and another ten and one here and one there and they have all come together and said: 'But we don't want that tree there'.

The Graven Hill Development Company was contacted but declined to comment.

# II

Graven Hill is a UK-version of Garreau's edge city,

but still a long way from the 'campus-like' existence with shops, cinemas, restaurants and cultural events served up on the sites Garreau documented. In fact, Bicester town council has asked Baker to encourage the residents of Graven Hill to feel they are part of the town, not *'apart'* from it.

Yet the same sense of 'self-containment' lies at its heart and with that in mind, Graven Hill could perhaps be viewed as an edge city in embryonic form. While for now, at least, Baker says, the people of Graven Hill consider the wider town as 'their main thoroughfare', that could change depending on how many and what kind of shops are opened on the site.

It could also be argued, that after Covid, both fitness and entertainment have already moved back to the home on Zoom.

Still in its larval form, the future of this community lies in the hands of the 'do-ers and makers' who are drawn to it. Whether it evolves into Britain's first true 'eco-burb' nestling on the edge of open countryside, or whether armies of commuter homes and retail developments are allowed to encroach and weaken its community strength, remains to be seen.

What is clear is that suburbia is being re-invented in myriad ways and with dazzling speed. And perhaps the most striking incarnation of it is Graven Hill.

# Chapter 6
## *Established edge city: Brent Cross*

We spent our lockdown visiting edge cities – three in particular which appear to be emerging, albeit slowly: Whiteley in Hampshire on the M27 outside Southampton, Birchwood in Cheshire on the M62 on the outskirts of Warrington, and Graven Hill in Oxfordshire on the M40, on the outskirts of Bicester.

All are on motorway junctions and, although they have a range of different origins – Whiteley began with a superstore, Birchwood with a science park and Graven Hill with a self-built housing development – they all three have a number of aspects in common. They all have a history of wartime or military occupation, which may allow developers to claim them as 'brownfield' development, rather than greenfield. They are all in a sense privately developed 'new communities' too, and aware of themselves as such.

Two of them have their own town councils. And Graven Hill clearly will have one at some point, because the current 'dictatorship of the developer' isn't sustainable. Only one of them straddles current local government boundaries – which is part of Garreau's original definition in the USA.

Two of them will have difficulties with over-heating: Bicester is now growing so fast that there will be difficulties with transport in the future, and similar difficulties threaten to overwhelm Whiteley with traffic.

Only Birchwood, part of the Warrington new town development, has enough public transport to make it reasonably liveable in the medium-term, with a railway station right by the shopping centre.

All in all, edge cities are clearly on the way here from the USA – but how American will they be, and how British? There is the key question. To find an answer, we consulted David Lock, a former planning advisor to environment ministers Chris Patten and John Gummer in the 1990s, and a former chair of the TCPA – Ebenezer Howard's old ginger group, the Town and Country Planning Association – and as such, an admirer of new settlements, new towns and garden cities (he now lives in Milton Keynes).

Lock sees things rather differently. He names the three key UK edge cities, which fit Joel Garreau's definition as:

- *Brent Cross*, an edge city 'happening before our

eyes'.

- He also says *Birmingham's NEC* area ("everyone's pretending it isn't one, but it is, actually," he says) – because of the scale of development there in terms of mixed-use and housing, the various museums there and the international train station – for Eurostar and where HS2 will come in.

- *Manchester's Trafford Centre*, because it started off as a regional shopping centre of a million square feet but is now diversifying by having lots of flats and all the other things that make it an edge city.

All three have been set up in competition with the city centre, or the 'core'. They have to fight the city core all the way, but they have the advantage of economic power behind them.

Lock also cited Sheffield's Meadow Hall and West Midland's Merry Hill.

Those are mature edge cities and they fit into a different category to ours. Lock said that none of our three places are edge cities as described in Garreau's book. Whiteley is just "urban sprawl extension", and the same goes for Birchwood – just a place where warehouses and storage depots have sprung up around motorway junctions because of the good accessibility for delivering or supplying goods.

As for Graven Hill, the new housing estates

around Bicester are so far away from Bicester they can't be considered to be on its 'edge'. Their geography in terms of their relation to Bicester is 'quite meaningless' and it is quicker for people living in those housing estates to get to Oxford or anywhere else.

Bicester, like Warwick, in other words, is just what he called a "huge area of housing estates".

Places like Graven Hill and other developments around Bicester are merely "a consequence of repression elsewhere in Oxfordshire". Bicester is only belatedly turning the last 'petal' of surrounding development into a 'green' development.

Looked at like that, neither Whiteley, Birchwood nor Graven Hill would be 'edge cities' because they are not essentially mixed-use places of work, residence, leisure, retailing and maybe some civic uses, as described in Joel Garreau's book thirty years ago. None have what it takes to make them small city centres located on the rim of a Mexican hat, which is what Garreau's book was talking about.

It hardly needs saying, but we are not sure Lock is quite right to dismiss them. The key element for UK edge cities is that they are on or near motorway junctions: Whiteley is on the rim of the hat with Southampton in the middle, just as Graven Hill has Bicester or Oxford in the middle and Birchwood has Warrington – or perhaps Liverpool and Manchester

– in the middle of various hats.

What makes the difference with the NEC outside Birmingham or Brent Cross is that they are edge cities at the earliest stages of development. Any motorway junction – whether it also sports an out-of-town shopping centre or an Amazon warehouse – has the tendency to grow and to become an edge city.

Still, we felt it was sensible to take a closer look at Brent Cross, which began as a shopping centre back in 1976.

# II

The shininess of the vast, gleaming retail halls in Brent Cross has now faded, the streets leading from the motorway turn-off shabby and neglected. A year ago (May 21) shoppers had to be evacuated when a 21-year-old man was stabbed to death.

But it is preparing once again to blaze a turbo-charged trail into the future by bagging 180 acres of former industrial land lying idle around its borders and transforming itself into Britain's first carbon net zero town by 2030.

The £7 billion regeneration project – the largest ever undertaken in the UK by a single developer – is as grand-scale and forward-thinking as those dreamt up for the site back in seventies. There will be 6,700 homes built centred around eight new public squares with access to 50 acres of parks and playing fields. Space for an expected 25,000 people to work on site is included, along with 50 shops and restaurants.

Brent Cross town has already been earmarked for a Skyport – a landing and take-off pad for drones and air taxis – expected to feed into a new global network of ports sited along drone superhighways. But until 'sky-hopping' becomes routine, travellers will arrive and depart on the Northern Line at Brent Cross and Brent Cross West, a Midland mainline Thameslink station, due to open at the end of this year.

Mindful of the post-Covid need for home working, there is room for a desk in every flat, free co-working areas in every block and fibre broadband in every home and office.

The developers have pledged to create a 'sense of place' by constructing town squares, green spaces, garden and parks. They are also working with Manchester University to develop a "flourishing index" to measure and track the happiness, health, productivity and neighbourliness of residents as the project develops. In the sales pavilion, there are artists' impressions of the lives of future residents as they switch from morning runs, to co-working spaces to drinks and tapas with friends – it is a vision that fits perfectly with Garreau's 'edge city' beliefs.

To Lock, it offers a clear-cut British blueprint of an American edge city – evidence that, long after they mushroomed across America, we are now turning to them in a post-Covid, post cost-of-living-crisis era. "It is the only site that comes close to an edge city in the south east, an area of mixed use that is happening before your eyes."

"We never had edge cities in quite the way the Americans had them, but we are now developing some 'edge situations' of intensification. The best examples are not, as some books would have it, Canary Wharf, because that's right in the middle of London and not on the edge – but we have 'edge situations 'like Brent Cross.'

# III

Before we leave the issue of what is happening now, we talked to geographer Olivier Sykes, a senior lecturer in 'European Spatial Planning Geography and Planning from Liverpool university. He is a convinced 'urbanist', so he takes a rather different line to David Lock. For example, he emphasises how different Europe is from the USA,

The question, for Olivier is whether edge cities are just an American planning concept or a real phenomenon. "There's the Manchester Airport City project – Airport City Manchester, for example, is a push around the Edge City concept," he says. "But is it a phenomenon? It's hard to define it."

Either way, he doesn't really like the UK version in practice. "If I want to see dystopia, I just have to travel out to the edges of St Helen's or Warrington and see lots of Barratt homes and Amazon warehouses, and it feels quite refreshing to return to civilisation after that. I'm from the countryside and I only like one or the other. But I'm not sure that it's quite the same as in the US, because they have 'zoning' and local planning there is quite different."

In France, for example, they have much smaller local authorities than they do here. "People think the UK is like an America but. in fact, the nature of suburban planning means that France is more like it – if you take areas like Lille, it has something like 79 local authorities across the urban area whereas we've got about five or six on a similar site and when you've got each one of those looking for a new Carrefour supermarket and a business park you do end up with something that looks superficially a lot more like the American system."

"There's a lot more neon in France around the edge of city centres," he says.

It was Sykes who suggested we visit Birchwood, in fact. "There are no pavements," he says. "Pavements don't follow the roads – it's classic 70s planning."

Where he does agree with Lock, it is around how the struggle between the centre and the periphery has been raging – back to the 1930s and John Betjeman's famous poem 'Come, friendly bombs and fall on Slough'.[11] Slough would have been a kind of edge city back then – and so would have so much of the development heading out of London to the West.

"Those Sunblest factories and Jacobs' biscuit factories are quite ancient - and that dates back a long time," he says. "There is probably a cultural shift as well among younger people – people like myself with a ten-year-old are now absolutely adamant about clinging on in the inner city. I reckon in the 70s or 80s, I would have been packing my bags and heading out to one of these estates by this stage. So the urban lifestyle is aspirational now in a way that it wasn't in my parents' generation. The people I work and study with – their parents fled the cities in the 1970s and 80s to move into places that look horrible to me, now. I wouldn't want to live there – they're just grim."

France, on the other hand, is the one country in Europe still decentralising, Nor did it have the same level of urban decline. "If you look at where stuff is going, it's not going back into a hole as much as was

---

[11] "Tinned fruit, tinned meat, tinned fish, tinned beans,/ Tinned minds, tined breath..."

created, which is more the case in Germany, the UK and to an extent the Netherlands. Maybe in the UK and the USA, the doughnut hollowed out. Whereas in France the city centres always retained more, says Olivier.

"With France, you can drive literally an hour from Paris and be in places that are unbelievable – and Paris is on its own. It isn't like the London thing that stretches up to God knows where – Nottingham? Where everywhere has got a Co-op and a Waitrose and is effectively a suburb of London. As soon as you are 40 miles outside Paris, the gaps between the spokes of the wheel and what is in between those spokes – there's nothing there."

It is true that compared to France, most places in England are just so busy.

There are so many unknowns about the future now. What should we put into high streets where the shops used to be? What happens to secondary retail centres in an era of online retail? What is going to happen to employment? Out of town shopping was the original challenge but it has been surpassed to some extent by online retail. How has Covid affected planning?

"The idea of edge cities is interesting," says Olivier. "It brings a lot of things into play such as transport, lifestyle and then patterns of employment as well because that is quite important.

"A student I knew lived in a place called Woodbridge in Illinois which is a suburb of Chicago, and it was 45 miles to the downtown – that's an insane scale of sprawl. If it was in England, places like Charlottesville in the USA would have sprawl stretching as far as Liverpool to Leeds."

The Canadian urbanist Charles Montgomery wrote about people working in San Francisco, but living two and a half hours' drive away from there – so that, if their child gets taken sick at nursery school, they have to drive a long way home.[12]

Garreau wrote about a time in the future when location no longer mattered in quite the same way. It maybe that, thanks to a combination of weariness with commuting and Covid, that is where we are heading. The issue for us is not whether edge cities are emerging in the UK, but how to make sure they stay liveable and humane.

--------------------------------

[12] Charles Montgomery (2015), *Happy City: Transforming Our Lives Through Urban Design,* London: Penguin.

# Chapter 7
## *Finale and conclusions*

David Lock described the phenomenon as nothing really new, even when Joel Garreau coined the phrase 'Edge Cities'. They have been there since the 1920s, and are created by powerful economic forces.

Lock used the Mexican hat analogy to explain this. City centres are the 'crown' of the hat, then there is an area prone to 'dereliction' between the crown and the rim. In the USA, this has helped to create some of the 'doughnut cities', like Dallas or Detroit. The rim or the 'edge' is where market forces and therefore development want to go, because land is cheap there and it is where people live – and there is good accessibility for delivery of goods to companies.

Edge cities were more common in America and, until now, we never had them here in 'quite the same way' because in the US there is no planning regulation to curb the drive to the edge. Without regulation, they sprang up spontaneously in the USA. Here, under UK planning regulations, there is a constant battle by the core to curb the drive to the edge, because it sees the threat from the edge draining its life blood away.

The growth of the edge would naturally be far greater but, until now, has been kept in check by our quite serious planning system, managing spatial distribution.

In Britain, the political imperative has always been to try to use brownfield land first – but it is expensive, the geography doesn't always suit people's lives. Nor is it always what the market wants.

Some areas don't even have any brownfield land – Cambridge, for example.

But – and this is an important *but*...

We are currently at an important juncture: planning laws are now very weak. There is a serious lack of expertise in the profession – many planning departments no longer have anyone even to answer the phones – and regional planning has been scrapped since David Cameron's premiership. Local authorities are expected to deal with their own development needs fifteen years ahead and thus forced to 'consume their own smoke'.

Worse, after Covid, the core is full of offices no one wants to be in and market forces, which are always champing at the edge of the Mexican hat, are now very strong at a time when there isn't really anywhere else for them to go in a lot of our towns and cities.

This is uncharted territory, and it is one reason

why edge cities are beginning to emerge. As well as all these factors, politicians will not be able to keep their promises to protect the green belt. All urban areas are bound to be under pressure at their edges.

This convergence of crises leads Lock to believe that carefully controlled edge cities could provide us with the UK's city of the future. "Edge city is beginning to grow as we speak," he says. "I think you will see that the pressure for edge situations to develop is resurging for economic reasons and will be so powerful..."

The other issue is whether this is a good thing at all. Garreau appeared to set out to how they were not – at least that is how popular culture understood him in the UK, but these days he is convinced that edge cities are inevitable.

In the USA, they appeared to host black people in particular, which is why they became the homes of the emerging new black middle class. It seemed to them to be a way to start afresh, without some of the continuing racism embedded in older places and institutions.

"And that isn't a bad thing always," says David Lock. "If you're converting urban malls into mixed use centres and it can be managed in scale, so that it doesn't drain the genuine heart of the city functions, then I think there's a case to be made for it to be managed that way here."

So here is the key element which needs to govern our attitude to our emerging edge cities in the UK. We need to ask ourselves the following questions. Have we got the right institutions to make sure they don't drain away the lion's share of the investment and the people from our city centres – as they have in the USA? And how do we steer away from 'slumburbia',[13] preventing the edges of our cities going the way of Paris and Glasgow, with hideous out of-town housing estates for the decanted poor – like Easterhouse or Seine-Saint-Denis?

We can certainly learn something from Peter Calthorpe's 1993 book *The Next American Metropolis* – which sets out the 'correct sequence' for development to follow:

1. *Downtown brownfields.* That should be the first priority – but brown should really mean previously developed. There is no point in building on urban parks.

2. *Edge of the city but only on public transport corridors,* as set out by Peter Hall and Colin Ward in

---

[13] See Sebastian Dembeki *et al* (2021), 'Reurbanisation and suburbia in Northwest Europe: A comparative perspective on spatial trends and policy approaches', *Progress in Planning,* Vol 150, Aug.

their update of Ebenezer Howard, *Social Cities*.[14]

3. *New hubs* – we would call them new towns or garden cities – on the public transport corridors far enough to be capable of being self-supporting but sufficiently connected to the centre for access to huge multi-scale facilities that can't be replicated in every town.

"The basic principles of all [towns]," wrote Calthorpe, "regardless of type or location, are simple. They must be mixed use, transit orientated, walkable and diverse. Reordering private space to make public space more useable, and the focus of each neighbourhood, is an overarching goal."[15]

Quite so...

# II

There are two new forces that are changing the picture. First, the evidence from the USA is that the out-of-town shopping era is now firmly over. We are

[14] Peter Hall and Colin Ward (1999). *Social Cities: The 21st-Century Reinvention of the Garden City,* Oxford: Blackwells.

[15] Peter Calthorpe (3rd edition, 1996) The *Next American Metropolis: Ecology, Community and the* American *Dream,* Princeton Architectural Press, 7.

beginning to awake from the great shopping mall dream – we have consumed and are now replete.

That seems to be the message of a 2014 book of photos by the American photographer Seph Lawless, dusty and crumbling, with dead ornamental trees at the foot of abandoned escalators. The first year since the 1950s with no new shopping malls built in the USA was 2007, and that was before the financial crash.[16]

We are behind that trend in the UK, but not far. Back in 2014, surprise figures showed that out of-town shopping centres were declining faster than high streets.[17] *Retail Gazette* in the UK has warned that "there is a danger that larger spaces will turn into empty buildings, with only tumbleweed passing through them".[18]

It wasn't what we expected. From 2003, one of us (David) was one of the small team at the New Economics Foundation on the Clone Town Britain campaign, a plaintive cry against everywhere looking the same.

---

[16] Seph Lawless (2nd edition, 2019, *Abandoned Malls of America: Crumbling Commerce Left Behind*, Racehorse.

[17] *Guardian* (2013), Sept 11.
https://www.theguardian.com/business/2013/sep/10/shopping-centres-retail-parks-high-street

[18] See *Retail Gazette* (2014), June.

It had enormous coverage and nearly two decades have passed since. But I don't think any of us guessed then that the clone town trend would be so short-lived – not because the small shops would succumb, but because of the euthanasia of the clones. A long list of them have since collapsed, from Woolworths to Virgin Megastores. So goodbye to Borders, Zavvi, Tower Records, JJB Sports, MFI.

How could we have so misunderstood? The answer is that, in most sectors, it's easier to go online and get stuff quickly and cheaply – maybe picking it up at a store, using "click and collect". If we don't know what we want, then a bit of convenient browsing tends to require old-fashioned bricks and mortar, preferably with a whiff of personality about them.

If it involves a couple of hours fuming on a motorway slip road near Bluewater, then really we have better things to do with our lives. The new retail laws suggest you need either be cheap (Lidl) or convenient (my corner store). You have to either be easy (Amazon) or authentic (the local bookshop). There is no obvious role for anything between, especially if it involves being peered at suspiciously by security guards or pushing trolleys down miles of identical aisles.

The modern mall began in Ohio in the 1920s and spread out in the 1950s. It was reinvented by the

American developer James Rouse, just as Brent Cross opened here, as a "festival marketplace" – shopping plus fun and spectacle. Its much more recent demise implies that investment and attention is going back onto local high streets. That is certainly what the UK intends.

It is increasingly clear that the two regions that invested most in out-of-town shopping – Wales and the north east – have, unsurprisingly perhaps, the most vacancies in their high streets.

This relatively new trend looks set to bring people back to ordinary high streets, and to shun their shiny, new out-of-town centres.

The other trend may take people the opposite way. After Covid, there are reasons why we have a revival of living in suburbs.

"There is a kind of creative freedom in the suburbs which sets the pace for self-expression," said Ged Pope, the author of *All the Tiny Moments Blazing: A Literary Guide to Suburban London.*[19] "This is expressed in gardens especially. A garden has currency now. Lots of people express themselves by growing plants, or it's somewhere where you can

---

[19] Ged Pope (2020) *All the Tiny Moments Blazing: A Literary Guide to Suburban London,* London: Reaktion Books. https://www.amazon.co.uk/All-Tiny-Moments-Blazing-Literary/dp/1789143071

recharge and observe nature."

He told the *Times* that cycling has brought new life to many London suburbs and dog ownership is helping to forge neighbourly relations and a new appreciation of traditional parks.[20]

*The New York Times* calls this reassessment of areas "hipsturbia", the transformation of a hitherto nondescript suburb into a suddenly cool location. Although Pinner may have a way to go, it has happened already in East Dulwich, says Pope, who has lived in the southeast London suburb for 20 years.

"The idea of the parade has come back. When I moved here in 2000, it was run-down. There was a shop that sold tyres, shops that sold basins, prams. But now we have two cheese shops, a deli, a French bakers, retro fish and chip shops. There no chains here either. We don't have a Gap or Starbucks. These are local one-off things, adding to the uniqueness."

Pope said that this lack of national chains, save for supermarkets — Waitrose and Sainsbury's are still prized, even with Ocado and Deliveroo — is a key marker between suburb and small town. He concedes

---

[20] Jayne Dowle (2021), 'The best suburbs to move to in the UK', *The Times,* Jun 1.
https://www.thetimes.co.uk/article/the-best-suburbs-to-move-to-in-the-uk-gfsmvs23l

that it can often be difficult to spot where one stops and the other begins.

Pope thinks that a British suburb is generally characterised by a train station, unlike the American suburb, largely reliant on the car. There are of course the planned Victorian and Edwardian "garden suburbs" such as Hampstead Garden Suburb in north London, Bournville in Birmingham, and Port Sunlight on the Wirral, the last two built by philanthropic industrialists.

Lucian Cook, the director of research at Savills property consultancy, predicts that some of the furthest-flung suburbs in cities including London, Newcastle, Birmingham, Leeds and Manchester will experience an unexpected renaissance, thanks to post-pandemic life and work adjustments.

"Suburbs could be set to see a further recovery in the next stage of the cycle as buyers continue to look for more space," he says. "Buyers might struggle to find that in the country given the intense competition in that market and seek to find the best of both worlds with good access to the countryside but the amenities of the urban environment."

Fast internet speeds are also a priority for the new suburban dweller, says Jeremy Leaf, a north London estate agent and a former Royal Institution of Chartered Surveyors (RICS) residential chairman. He is starting to see people who fled central London during Covid to rent in the countryside "drifting back towards the outer suburbs for more permanent accommodation" instead of heading back to grittier postcodes.

Suburbs orbit almost every sizeable city in the UK. Cook cites Ponteland West in Newcastle (£507,627), Fulwood in Sheffield (£569,371) and Sutton Four Oaks in Birmingham (£760,366) for proximity to good schools, green space and countryside, decent transport links andchigh-quality housing stock. Middle class Alwoodley in north Leeds (£501,821) and Westbury-on-Trym and Henleaze (£683, 161), well-placed between Bristol and the River Severn, are also highlighted.

Other standouts — and regulars in *The Sunday Times* Best Places to Live guide — include family-friendly Harborne, elegant Edgbaston and upwardly mobile Solihull in Birmingham.

Woolton and Allerton head the pack in Liverpool, but also don't forget West Kirby on the Wirral, where the veteran children's writer and illustrator Shirley Hughes found inspiration in red-brick semis with long gardens. Mapperley Park in Nottingham and Penart ana Pontcanna in Cardiff are already well established and favoured by families and young professionals. As are the *uber*-desirable "seaside suburbs", like Crosby on Mersey-side, Tynemouth near Newcastle and Portobello in Edinburgh.

Then there are the villages that refuse to be called suburbs. Natalie Simpson, the head of Strutt & Parker in Edinburgh, emphasises that suburbs such as Ratho Village are considered villages.

"The past year has seen those who may have previously stayed in the centre of Edinburgh head out to the suburbs such as Ratho Village in search of more space, mainly families, freeing up more central property for first-time buyers and upsizers," she says. "For Edinburgh the benefits of this have been huge, creating a great property cycle for the market."

Nor do people want to commute any more if they can possibly avoid it.

Attitudes, too, are changing, as noted by young *Times* columnist James Marriott in August last year titled: 'My generation does not sneer at the suburbs'.[21] He saw the middle classes beginning a great migration back to Metroland away from sterile city centres.

Yet just because people *can* work from home, it doesn't mean they are always going to want to, wrote Professor Nick Gallant, from the Bartlett School of Architecture and Planning at University College,

---

[21]    https://www.thetimes.co.uk/article/my-generation-doesnt-sneer-at-the-suburbs-67dtc0g5j

London, in a recent article.[22]

"For many workers, the novelty of centring their lives at home, rolling out of bed and working in their pyjamas, or 'top dressing', has simply worn off," he wrote. "They want to reinstate the separation of work and home life, see colleagues again, meet people over lunch, and so on."

He is right that there are indications of a 'back to the city trend' but it isn't clear yet how strong this will be. In London. he reports that house prices are still falling in central areas like Westminster and the City, but – with the exception of Wandsworth– zone 3 suburb prices are rising again,

What all these various trends have in common is that they both will be driving people to shops near where they live. That is one reason why they are building homes at Brent Cross.

But the edge city phenomenon implies also that there will be more new built places too, near places for work built around motorway exits and junctions. So we suspect that the current boom in mega-shed building in the UK may turn out to be significant.

Knight Frank & Rutley said that – by the end of the year 2021 – 37m square feet of new distribution

[22] Nick Gallant (2022), 'Back to the city? What are the implications for rural areas?' *Town & Country Planning,* Vol 91, No 3, May-June.

and data centre floorspace would have been built – nearly twice what was built in 2019.[23]

Amazon now has distribution centres near Darlington, Gateshead, Leeds, Mansfield, Swindon and Dartford. The UK has the second biggest data hub in the world, after Virginia, around the M25. Gateshead Amazon is one of the biggest at 2.5m square foot.

We would take a bet that the big grey warehouse will not be the last application for planning that will be received for many – if not most – of these distribution centres.

# III

Because of Covid, we are seeing more of a kind of modern 'flight to the green', just as we experienced for most of the twentieth century.

There is nothing wrong with that idea. On the contrary, it means that people are yearning for calmness, greenery and community in their lives. It means they want the space to breathe, and the time

---

[23] Julia Kollewe and Rob Davies (2021), 'Online shopping revolution drives huge boom in UK megasheds', *The Guardian,* Aug 12.

too – they don't want to spend hours commuting every day. They want to live near where they work, and they want to shop near where they live – preferably using small locally-owned businesses. Which may be why recent research suggests that people living outside cities are happier than those inside them.[24]

All we would suggest is that politicians will still need to find ways of helping poorer people to leave the cities too – otherwise they will be the only people still living in the old cities.

For that reason, we believe that the proto edge cities we visited for this book may be a model – as long as they can learn from each other. For example, they need to learn how to avoid getting so dependent on motor traffic that everything just seizes up.

They also need to develop some measure of local democracy, because without that they will hardly be sustainable.

# IV

So what is an edge city in the UK? We found it could

---

[24] Okulicz-Kozaryn, A. (2022) 'Unhappy Metros: Panel Evidence' *Applied Research Quality of Life*. https://doi.org/10.1007/s11482-022-10102-7

be many things – from a regenerated military base nestled on the border of city expanse to a trading depot sited on a host of arterial transport links, where people have settled, bringing with them civilising architecture, to a gathering of the like-minded inspired to build homes and a community from scratch with new ecological awareness.

In fact, it isn't the buildings themselves. It is the concept of apart-ness that defines the 'edge' in edge cities, the appeal of the notion of nestling cosily beside the centre of things while enjoying a sense of independent community and identity.

It may also be where our future lies.

# Lesley Yarranton
# *Saving Munich 1945:*
# The story of Rupprecht Gerngross

It is nearly thirty years since I first heard of a small group of German army officers rising up against Hitler to save Munich in the dying days of the Nazi regime.

I was a foreign correspondent, who had moved to Berlin within days of the Wall being torn down, and had been tracking the rise of neo-Nazi groups starting to flourish in covert, underground cells across the forlorn expanses of the defunct, communist German Democratic Republic.

Most were bunches of disenfranchised, shorn-headed youths, brought together by a lethal cocktail of nostalgia for the glories of Germany's past and hostility to what they saw as greedy western corporations rushing to profit from cheap land, a cheap workforce and the undamming of a large market of hungry consumers.

One group, led by a former member of the German Freedom Movement *(Die Deutsche Freiheits-bewegung)*, was beginning to emerge as an umbrella organisation for multiple underground neo-Nazi splinter movements.

It stood out with its sophisticated *modus operandi*: slick corporate e-mails and "business headquarters" in an affluent suburb of Munich.

It did not take too much digging to gain access to Bela Ewald Althans: he was to be found at a meeting promoting the work of David Irving, the controversial right-wing British historian at the centre of the Goebbels' diaries row (Irving had been banned from Germany for "reasons of state security" and Althans was acting as his agent, smuggling him in and out of the country to give talks to spread the word about how the Holocaust was nothing but a 'great lie').

Saying he feared the possibility of a bomb attack at his office, Althans insisted on conducting the interview at his apartment. It was an interview I will never forget. Perched on the edge of a chair in a modest flat in an ordinary Munich street, I listened as Althans, an imposing six foot figure, dressed head-to-toe in black, talked darkly about his plans for the movement.

We sat for over an hour, surrounded by framed

photographs of Hitler and Nazi memorabilia while, in a corner of the dimly-lit room, black and white footage from Third Reich movie-maker Leni Riefenstahl's fawning productions flickered silently on a loop.

He talked calmly and confidently but grew agitated when I asked him about his decision to base his movement in Munich, rather than in the new capital of Berlin. Was it influenced by the loyalty Munich had historically shown to Hitler?

Yes, he said, it was the city that had proudly supported the Führer but – at the end – "even in this loyal city" Hitler had been betrayed. One young captain had "shamelessly" turned his own soldiers and led military units against the regime in the last days of the war in a bid to force an early surrender. The timing, he argued, was the worst humiliation.

The *coup* staged by the young captain was brief – the American forces entered the city just days later - but it was a story I had never heard before. The Stauffenberg 'Valkyrie' plot to assassinate Hitler with a bomb was well-known. This was very different. The idea of younger, lesser-ranking rebels challenging the Führer at his deluded end was fascinating. What happened to them?

I hastily scribbled a note in the margin of my notebook but my searches for reports of the young captain the next day drew a blank and I began to doubt the accuracy of what I had been told. A news editor's summons sent me back to Berlin and I dismissed them from my thoughts.

But nearly thirty years later, upon reading historian David Boyle's revelations of the furious struggle in and around the BBC over wartime broadcasting and its controversial sacking of the man in charge of European news, a figure sprang out of its pages like a ghost from the past.

Noel Newsome, the BBC's director of European broadcasts, had heard of a group of German soldiers turning against the Nazis, seizing the state broadcasting station to launch a general uprising and fighting the SS on the streets. The young captain's broadcasts had been recorded and reported on by the BBC.

Newsome had interviewed Captain Rupprecht Gerngross. He had helped to save the city of Munich and many of the lives of the 400,000 people still living there.

He filed an in-depth account to the *Times* newspaper only for it never to appear. It had been pulled from the presses at the last moment after a newspaper executive sent it to the Foreign Office to be 'vetted for policy'. It was rejected on the grounds that it was "not thought desirable to suggest that there were 'good Germans'". As a result, Newsome's account, written in 1945, could not be read until

2018, when his autobiography was finally published.

The reason why my efforts to find information about Gerngross and his men all those years ago had proved so difficult, soon became clear. Their story had lain untold because it served as a reminder of painful, war-end humiliations, highlighted people's own failure to act and, for the most part, wasn't believed.

It took research from material released to archives following the death of Gerngross in 1996 – and Newsome's account – for a more forgiving evaluation of the rebellion to quietly emerge from decades of suppression. It has led to, what some would argue, is the long, overdue erection or restoration of monuments in small towns and villages across Bavaria commemorating the German soldiers, who tore the Nazi regalia from their uniforms and died fighting Nazis.

This, finally, is their story.....

*Carry on reading, buy or download the book from TheRealPress.co.uk or from Amazon…*

# David Boyle
# *Cancelled*
## *The strange, disturbing story of the Southern Railways crisis – and what we can do about it*

*"As a long-serving @southernrail commuter, finally radicalised by absurd circumstance, I would like to thank you."*
**Tweet sent to me after the blogs I wrote.**

The American anthropologist Polly Wiessner used to argue that the sense of reciprocity, which she studied for decades among the !Kung bushmen in southern Africa, was part of the wiring for us human beings. If she is right, we are hard-wired for give and take.

We may not fully remember this but, when it gets betrayed – when we are let down, as we so often are by the companies we shop with – we feel extremely angry. More angry than perhaps the situation demands.

In the middle of the strange collapse of Southern rail services to Sussex in the summer of 2016, I remembered this and wondered. There I was on Hayward's Heath station, when hundreds of people – maybe thousands of people around me – were showing signs, unusual in the English, of absolute rage.

The third train to the coast had been cancelled. More trains were arriving, and being cancelled, as mine had been. More people were pouring onto the already crowded platform, their faces set – the sign that the English are very unhappy indeed. "This is exactly what happened last Thursday," said a woman next to me. "This is the third train cancelled today that I've been on," said another one. "That's another evening ruined by Southern Rail."

The staff in their yellow, fluorescent jackets were calm as they directed furious passengers from platform to platform, and advised them to go via Brighton. I had already heard, at that stage, about conditions in Brighton and how the police were directing rows of shuffling, disaffected passengers trying to get trains along the coast which no longer existed. It was not a tempting prospect.

"This fucking train company," a man was saying into his mobile phone, and it was clear – in so many words – that's what other passengers were thinking too. A train rumbled into the empty platform behind us and stopped. On impulse, I tore at the door, trying to open it with my fingers. You get desperate sometimes when you are tired and trying to get home. "This train is not stopping here," said the tannoy, in flagrant defiance of the basic facts.

"You can't do that," said a somewhat supercilious despatch staff member. "If you succeed, you'll break the door, and the train will be stuck." In fact, of course, it was me that was stuck again.

The Southern Railways crisis had increased another notch that night. Of their regular trains on the Southern network, people trying to get home to their families, up to a third had been cancelled. It was hardly surprising that people were cross, as cross as the English can get when they are let down so badly by the services they pay for. Suddenly, there was another flurry of activity. The train to the coast was moving slowly into the station. It looked dangerously full.

A pregnant woman ahead of me looked faint as she squeezed on. There was no question of reaching a seat. I was forced to calm a spat that broke out between two irritable passengers, one of whom was calling the other a "do-gooder". Like this, squeezed into this tiny space in unwilling intimacy with other members of the human race, we crawled down to the coast. Again.

Those kinds of journeys do happen sometimes, especially in the UK where the underinvestment in equipment and manpower has been chronic. But this had been the same for weeks, and appeared to be getting worse. I wrote a short blog about one conversation I had with rail staff, only to find that it had been read by more than 70,000 people in a few days. By then, the proportion of trains between London and Brighton and arriving within five minutes of their scheduled time had dropped to just 13 per cent, frustrated passengers were holding demonstrations outside the Brighton terminus. Even in leafy, respectable South Croydon, passengers abandoned on the platform were chanting: "Where are the trains! Where are the trains!"

The whole experience made me insanely cross. Then, when the number of people reading my blog tipped over 3,000 an hour, rather scared. So many people responded with letters, comments and emails, that I suddenly knew a great deal more about Southern Railways and its unravelling than I had done a few days before. I run a small publishing enterprise. I believe that publishing should respond to the moment, and I felt this was an opportunity for me to show what I meant about reinventing the way publishing worked. I would find out what was really going on and use the information I had been sent by literally hundreds of people caught up in the same affair. This is, after all, a far more serious and, in some ways, more frightening series of events than they seemed at first.

They also have important implications for the way we live. That is why I have written this book. I hope that, by explaining what is really going on, and suggesting things we might do about it, that I will have been able to make a small difference. Not least of which, a small difference to my train journeys to London and back...

*Carry on reading, buy or download the book from TheRealPress.co.uk or from Amazon...*

96

www.ingramcontent.com/pod-product-compliance
Lightning Source LLC
Chambersburg PA
CBHW021935040426
42448CB00008B/1079